Seasons

Spring

Siân Smith

Heinemann Library
Chicago, Illinois

Editorial: Rebecca Rissman, Charlotte Guillain, and Siân Smith
Picture research: Elizabeth Alexander and Sally Claxton
Designed by Joanna Hinton-Malivoire
Printed and bound in China by Leo Paper Group

13 12 11 10 09
10 9 8 7 6 5 4 3 2

ISBN-13: 978-1-4329-2728-8 (hc)
ISBN-13: 978-1-4329-2733-2 (pb)

Library of Congress Cataloging-in-Publication Data

Smith, Siân.
  Spring / Siân Smith.
    p. cm. -- (Seasons)
  Includes bibliographical references and index.
  1. Spring--Juvenile literature. I. Title.
  QB637.5.S65 2008
  508.2--dc22
                          2008049156

Acknowledgments

The author and publisher are grateful to the following for permission to reproduce copyright material:
©Alamy pp.**8** (Adam Burton), **11** (Alistair Heap), **7** (Andrew Cowin), **21** (Arco Images GmbH), **17** (Nature Online); ©Corbis pp.**16, 10** (amanaimages/Steve Cole), **20** (Brakefield Photo/Brand X), **04 br** (Image100), **14, 23 top** (John Aikins), **18** (Julie Habel), **9** (Mark Karrass), **5** (Momatiuk-Eastcott), **13, 23 middle top** (Papilio/Steve Austin), **19** (Sygma/Andre Fatras), **04 tl** (Zefa/Roman Flury); ©Getty Images pp.**12, 23 bottom** (Bob Thomas), **04 tr** (Floria Werner); ©iStockphoto.com pp.**6, 23 middle bottom** (Bojan Tezak), **04 bl** (Inga Ivanova); ©Photodisc p.**15** (Lifelife/Andrew Ward); ©Shutterstock p.**22** (Katerina Havelkova).
Cover photograph of purple and yellow crocus reproduced with permission of ©Gap Photos Ltd (J S Sira). Back cover photograph reproduced with permission of ©Corbis (Mark Karrass).

Every effort has been made to contact copyright holders of any material reproduced in this book. Any omissions will be rectified in subsequent printings if notice is given to the publisher.

Contents

What Is Spring?

spring

summer

fall

winter

There are four seasons every year.

Spring is one of the four seasons.

When Is Spring?

spring

summer

winter

fall

The four seasons follow a pattern.

Spring comes after winter.

The Weather in Spring

It can be warm in spring.

It can rain in spring.

What Can We See in Spring?

In spring we can see people
in raincoats.

In spring we can see people in boots.

seed

In spring we can see people in gardens.

12

buds

In spring we can see buds.

In spring we can see blossoms.

In spring we can see flowers.

In spring we can see new plants starting to grow.

In spring we can see new leaves starting to grow.

In spring we can see eggs in nests.

In spring we can see chicks in nests.

In spring we can see baby animals.

In spring we can see hedgehogs
waking up.

Which Season Comes Next?

Which season comes after spring?

Picture Glossary

 **blossoms** flowers on trees

 **bud** part of a plant. Leaves or flowers come out of buds.

 **pattern** happening in the same order

 **seed** plants make seeds. Seeds grow into new plants.

Index

Note to Parents and Teachers
Before reading
Talk to the children about the four seasons of the year: spring, summer, fall, winter. Ask the children when their birthdays are and tell them which season their birthday falls in. Explain that spring is the season when things start to grow after the cold period of winter.

After reading
Make a seed head. Collect plastic mini yogurt containers and wash them thoroughly. Fill each pot with potting compost. Sprinkle grass seeds into the soil and then moisten the soil with cold water. Using colored paper cut out eyes, a nose and a mouth and glue them onto the pots. Leave the pots on the window sill in the sun. Add water if the soil dries out. Watch as the "hair" grows.